JEWS, GENTILES AND THE CHURCH AGE

The Jew And Christian Theology

Kenneth G. Symes

JEWISH AWARENESS MINISTRIES INC.
P.O. Box 706
Ramseur, NC 27316

www.xulonpress.com

TABLE OF CONTENTS

ϑϑ

INTRODUCTION

§§

Over and over, as I have both read and listened to sermons on radio, TV and cassettes, I have heard the phrase "The Gentile Church" or "The Gentile Church Age". To suggest that the church age is depicted as Gentile is to state that the Jews have been set aside until the Gentile church is completed. It also further suggests that the Jews cannot be saved in this church age.

Today there is much confusion among Christians as to the place which God has given to the Jew in this present age of Grace. Some people continue to teach that because this is "the time of the Gentiles" God has set the Jew aside while He is calling out a people from among the Gentiles for His Name. Many otherwise able Bible teachers speak of a "Gentile Church" when that expression is to be found nowhere in the Bible!

The Roman Catholic Church has traditionally taught that Jews are now cast off by God.

Unfortunately, this concept goes back to the time when Constantine professed to become a Christian. After making that profession he demanded that all people in his kingdom become Christians and be baptized. For those who refused, death was threatened. When most of the Jewish community refused, Constantine demanded that the Church expunge from its teachings any connection to Judaism whatsoever! Unfortunately, the church leaders acquiesced. The Church as we know it today has been, to a very large degree, affected by this decision of the early church fathers. How many Bible Colleges and Seminaries preparing men for the Gospel ministry have even one course on the Jewish Roots of the Christian Faith? How many teach that understanding the Jewish customs and traditions are important to really grasping the truth of God's Word, to truly understanding the message? It has only been in recent decades that pastors have begun to wear out their Old Testament as quickly as they wear out their New Testament!

Understanding the Jewish roots of the Christian faith is still the strongest defense against Biblical error and anti-Semitism. Dr. Charles Stevens, who was President of Piedmont Bible College, in his booklet, entitled *What It Has Cost The Church To Withhold Christ From The Jews*, states: "Had the Church through the ages maintained an effort to win the Jew to Christ, she would never have suffered such doctrinal extremes as are commonly found today. The church would have been saved from many wild and extravagant interpretations, nearly all of which grew out of the false idea of the Gentile Church with a kingdom-building program."

This book is a study of the relationship of the Jew to the Church and its effect on Christian theology. What does the Bible teach about the church age, the "Times of the Gentiles," the fullness of the Gentiles and the place of the Jew in it all? Perhaps the place to begin this journey is with the question, "What is the Church according to scripture?" Then, after coming to an understanding of the Church and the church age, perhaps the other issues will come together for us.

CHAPTER ONE

WHAT IS THE CHURCH?

The Word "church" in Greek is *Ecclesia*, a called-out assembly. In the pre-Christian era *ecclesia* was used to describe a regular assembly of the whole body of citizens in a free city-state who were called out by the herald for the discussion and decision of public business. The comparable Hebrew term is *kahal* and is used of the congregation of Israel (cf. Lev. 16: 15). To the Greek it suggested a self-governing, democratic society; to the Jew a theocratic society whose members were the subject of the heavenly King.

The first use of the term is found in Matthew 16:18. *"And I say also unto thee, that thou art Peter, and upon this rock I will build my church."* It appears that what Jesus had in mind was a body associated with His words *"the kingdom"*. Note three concepts here. The *ecclesia* consists of those confessing Jesus to be the Christ. The "rock" of which Jesus speaks in verse 16 is the confession that Jesus is the Christ. In I Cor. 10: 4, while speaking of the Jew's deliverance from Egypt Paul stated: *"And did all drink the same spiritual drink: for they drank of that spiritual Rock that followed them; and that Rock was Christ,"* thus indicating that the "rock" is a type of Christ. Messiah (Heb.) and Christ (Greek) are one and the same. The Hebrew Scriptures (OT) openly teach that Messiah is God. He is spoken of as the Son of God in Proverbs 30: 4 and Psalm 2: 7. Messiah is described as the sinless Son of God in Isaiah 50: 5-9 and Isaiah 53: 11. He is clearly God in Micah 5: 2 and Isaiah 9:6. But the clearest reference is found in Zechariah 12: 10. *"And I will pour upon the house of David, and upon the inhabitants of Jerusalem, the spirit of grace and of supplications: and they shall look upon me whom they have pierced, and shall mourn for him, as one mourneth for his only son."* In verse 9 Zechariah states: *"I will seek to destroy all the nations that come against Jerusalem."* Could Zechariah do that? Of course not! But who could? The "I" here can only be God Himself. Thus the "I" in verse 10 can only be God. Thus to confess Jesus to be the Christ (Messiah) is to confess Him to be God! John, in defining an overcomer, a born-again believer, wrote: *"Who is he that overcometh the world, but he that believeth that Jesus is the Son of God?"* (I Jn. 5: 5). Apart from the recognition of the deity of Jesus one cannot be saved. This is the foundational truth upon which the Church is built and all spiritual blessings flow.

Second, this new society was to be a representation of the heavenly kingdom realized on earth. This is the essence of the first phrase of verse 19. *And I will give unto thee the keys of the kingdom of heaven..."* The idea of the keys is that it takes a Peter-like faith in Jesus to be admitted into the Kingdom of Heaven. As we have already seen in I John 5: 5 no one can be saved apart from recognizing that Jesus is God.

Third, in the new society the righteousness of the Kingdom was to be found. This is the message of the last part of verse 19. *"And whatsoever thou shalt bind on earth shall be bound in heaven: and whatsoever thou shalt loose on earth shall be loosed in heaven."* The proclamation of God's Word through faithful men should be received as such: God's Word. Paul informed us that: *"We all, with open face beholding as in a glass the glory of the Lord, are changed into the same image from glory to glory even as by the Spirit of the Lord."* (II Cor. 3: 18). This is a process that begins the moment we are saved and does not end until we are called home to be with Him. We are called to holiness (Rom. 12:1). It is accomplished through *"the renewing of your mind."* (Rom. 12:2). This occurs through obedience to God's Word. The Church body, then, is called to demonstrate the righteousness of God's Kingdom.

Thus we see that the Church is constituted of believers in Yeshua (Jesus) whose lives have been transformed thereby. Is this faith that gives entrance into the *ecclesia* limited to Gentiles only? If so, the disciples could not have been a part of the Church, nor could Paul, because they were Jewish. Paul makes very clear that the Church is constituted of both Jew and Gentile. He stated: *"For he is our peace, who* *hath made both one, and hath broken down the middle wall of partition between us; having abolished in his flesh the enmity, even the law of commandments contained in the ordinances; for to make in himself of twain one new man, so making peace; and that he might reconcile **both** unto God in **one** body by the cross."* (Eph. 2: 14-16). Paul goes on to further state in verse 18: *"For through him we **both** have access by one Spirit unto the Father."* Obviously, the Church, according to Paul, is constituted of both Jew and Gentile.

Thus the early Church leaders preached the Gospel *"to the Jew first and also to the Greek"* in every town to which they went. Herein God set the pattern for the scriptural method of evangelism. No other approach has ever been divinely authorized. Thus, any method which leaves out God's order *"to the Jew first"* is in direct disobedience to His clearly stated will. Today there are many who suggest that this is not God's plan for today. They contend "first" does not mean first. In Acts 13:46 we read: *"Then Paul and Barnabas waxed bold, and said, it was **necessary** that the word of God should first have been spoken to you...."* The Greek word translated "necessary" is "anagkaios". Webster's unabridged dictionary defines "necessary" as "required, mandatory, not voluntarily." Some apply this in an historical framework and say that is precisely what happened. As the Gospel was shared with the Jews first in the first century, they teach that we are no longer under any obligation to do so now. That does seems to be the sense in this particular verse until you consider it within its context. All it says is that Paul and Barnabas shared the Gospel with the Jews first and then turned to the Gentiles. Herein was the example set! As did the early believers with their generation, so are we obligated to do the same for our generation. Is that not Paul's point in Romans 1:16?

The Greek word translated "first" both here and in Romans 1:16 is "proton" which denotes "in time, place, order or importance." This word is used 57 times. It is clear, if you trace the references, that it denotes order or importance each time it is used (cf. Matt. 5: 24, 6: 33, 7: 5, 8: 21 etc.). If the early Church shared the gospel with the Jews of their generation first, setting the example, was not Paul instructing that their example be followed by us as well?

William R. Newell, in his Romans commentary, regarding Rom. 1:16 stated: "To claim that the Gospel must be preached first to the Jew throughout this dispensation, is utterly to deny God's Word that there is now no distinction between Jew and Greek either as to the fact of sin (Rom. 3:22) or availability of salvation (Rom. 10:12)."[1] In actuality, the very opposite is true. It is the same Gospel that saves both Jew and Greek (Gentile)! The Gospel is for all, the same Gospel on the same terms but without prejudice to the historical prerogative of the Jews.

Another author suggested that to take Romans 1:16 literally conflicts with Galatians 3:28 which states: *"There is neither Jew nor Greek, there is neither bond nor free, there is neither male nor female: for ye are all one in Christ Jesus."* There is no conflict here!

Paul simply states that we are all treated the same way in Christ. Would this author deny that there are men and women in the world today? Of course not! In this passage Paul is speaking of the Church, the saved. In Romans 1:16 Paul is not speaking of the Church. He is describing the <u>lost</u>; those who need to hear the Gospel. To deny our responsibility to take the Gospel to the Jew is to deny God's Word.

Those who want to make the Church a "Gentile" Church often quote Acts 15:14. *"Simeon hath declared how God at the first did visit the Gentiles, to take out of them a people for his name."* First, understand that "Simeon" is the Hebrew form of the Greek "Simon". In other words, this is Peter. Taken in its context, James is simply stating that, according to Peter, the direct reception of Gentiles into the body (the Church) was no new thing introduced by Paul and Barnabas, but was practiced long before by Peter with divine approval. James affirms that this was a part of the divine plan from the beginning, as attested by the prophets of the Old Testament, especially those who predicted the first coming of Messiah (cf. Isa. 11:10; 42: 1-6; 49: 6; etc.). Simply stated, James proclaimed that the calling out of the Gentiles agrees with God's promises to Israel. The issue here was not: "Should there be a Gentile Church?" but whether or not Gentiles should be included in the Church. This verse, then, teaches the very opposite of a Gentile Church. The decision of the Church fathers was that Gentiles should be included, but not to the exclusion of the Jews. This is fully in line with Paul's teaching in Romans 11: 13-18 where he teaches that it is the

Gentiles who are grafted into the true faith of the Jews, not the reverse.

The Church, then, by scriptural definition is a group of people, Jewish and Gentile, called out by the exercising of faith in Jesus as God's Son who became the atonement sacrifice for their sins (Eph. 2: 14-16). The Church is to represent the Kingdom of Heaven on earth exemplifying the righteousness of that Kingdom. The primary purpose of the Church is to proclaim the Gospel message *to the Jew first and also to the Greek* that many, both Jew and Gentile, might believe and thus be brought into the kingdom. We are commanded to take the Gospel to **both** Jew and Gentile. It is also essential that the Church exemplify God's righteousness and holiness (cf. Matt. 6:33). To be "righteous" is to be obedient to God's clear commands. Yet today few local fellowships have any concern for reaching out to Jewish people with the Gospel let alone actually doing it! We are clearly commanded to take the Gospel to **all** people. And that includes the Jew. If you do not have Jewish people in your outreach area you should at least be supporting a solid biblical ministry to the Jews.

Regarding the Church "age", though Jesus laid the foundation for the Church before Pentecost, most would agree that the Church age began with the Church's empowerment by the Holy Spirit on the Jewish holy day of Pentecost as recorded in Acts chapter two and that it concludes with the rapture just before the beginning of Daniel's seventieth week. Those who become believers during the Tribulation (Daniel's 70th week) are never called "the Church", only "tribulation saints" (cf. Rev. 7:14). Is understanding the phrases "The times of the Gentiles" and "the fullness of the Gentiles" as teaching a Gentile Church consistent with the biblical definition of *ecclesia* (the church)? Apparently not! Let us consider further evidence.

CHAPTER TWO

THE TIMES OF THE GENTILES

§§

What is meant by the phrase "The times of the Gentiles"? One often thinks of the book of Daniel in relation to this phrase. However, it is not used in Daniel at all. The phrase is found only in Luke 21: 24. *"And they shall fall by the edge of the sword, and shall be led away captive into all nations: and Jerusalem shall be trodden down of the Gentiles, until the times of the Gentiles be fulfilled."* Here it is Israel (the Jewish people, not the Church) of whom Jesus speaks. Thus Jesus defines the "Times of the Gentiles" as that period in which Jerusalem would be under the dominion of Gentiles, not the Jews. Most Bible scholars believe this time began with the fall of Jerusalem to the Babylonians and will conclude with the Second Coming of Israel's Messiah, the Lord Jesus, when He will finally put down all of Israel's enemies and rule on David's throne from Jerusalem.

This period is best described for us in the book of Daniel in Nebuchadnezzar's dream of the image and Daniel's vision of the beasts (Daniel chapters 2 and 7).

According to Daniel, during this time there will be four great world empires: Babylon, Medo-Persia, Greece, and Rome. The first three kingdoms are history. Each was absorbed by its successor. However, Rome, in its original form, was never absorbed by another world power. It just rotted away. Thus the judgment prophesied upon this kingdom has yet to be fulfilled. The scriptures teach that in its final form the Roman Empire will be a ten-nation confederacy that is finally destroyed, not absorbed, at the time of the Second Coming when Messiah will establish the Millennial Kingdom (Dan. 2:42; 7: 7,24; Rev. 13: 1; 17: 12). Therefore the fulfillment of this prophecy must yet be future.

Thus, the phrase "The Times of the Gentiles" relates to God's dealings with the Gentile Nations. Though the four primary nations are used as divine instruments of judgment upon Israel, this is a time when God judges the Gentiles in relation to their dealings with Israel. The Old Testament prophets anticipated the judgment of the Gentile Nations. *"Therefore wait ye upon me, saith the LORD, until the day that I rise up to the prey: for my determination is to gather the nations, that I may assemble the kingdoms, to pour upon them mine indignation, even all my fierce anger: for all the earth shall be devoured with the fire of my jealousy."* (Zeph. 3:8). Read also Psalm 2: 1-10; Isaiah 63: 1-6; Joel 3: 2-16; and Zechariah

14: 1-3. In Matthew 25: 41 Jesus Himself speaks of the judgment of the opposing Gentile nations: *"Then shall he say also unto them on the left hand, depart from me, ye cursed, into everlasting fire, prepared for the devil and his angels."* This period of political Gentile history comes to a conclusion when the final form of Gentile political power (the revived Roman Empire) is crushed by the *"stone cut without hands."* (Dan. 2:34). This will occur at the Second Coming of the Messiah!

It is clear that the sense of the phrase *"The times of the Gentiles"* is not ecclesiastical (related to the Church) but political (related to the nations). Nowhere in scripture is this phrase used to describe the spiritual ascendancy of Gentiles over the Jews. Thus it cannot honestly be used to demonstrate the validity of a "Gentile" Church. Nor can it justly be used for anti-Semitic purposes as some have attempted to do. Therefore the phrase "The times of the Gentiles" neither describes nor teaches a Gentile Church or Gentile Church age.

CHAPTER THREE

THE FULLNESS OF THE GENTILES

ॐॐ

If the phrase "The times of the Gentiles" does not teach a Gentile Church or Gentile Church age, then surely the phrase "The fullness of the Gentiles" does indicate a Gentile Church. This phrase is found only in Romans 11:25. *"For I would not, brethren, that ye should be ignorant of this mystery, lest ye should be wise in your own conceits; that blindness in part is happened to Israel, until the fullness of the Gentiles be come in."*

If we are to correctly understand this verse we must first understand the context. Paul is writing to a very specific predominantly Gentile Church (cf. verse 13), the Church in Rome. Lest they become "high-minded" (Rom, 11:20) or "wise in their own conceits," Paul reminds them that God is not yet finished with Israel (the nation). The whole thought here is related to how God is, in this age, dealing with

Israel. Remember, God's dealings, up to this point with the Jewish people have been national. Israel, during the Church age, is set aside nationally while God speaks to both Jew and Gentile individually. The "blindness" of which Paul speaks in this verse is the blindness of national Israel that is the result of their national sins of idolatry and rebellion. God spoke of this national blindness to Isaiah when He sent him to proclaim His message to Israel (cf. Isa. 6:9, 10). This was a national blindness as is clearly indicated in Isaiah 6:11, 12. *"Then said I, Lord, how long? And He answered, until the cities be wasted without inhabitant, and the houses without man, and the land be utterly desolate, and the LORD have removed men far away, and there be a great forsaking in the midst of the land."* The context is clear. These verses are talking about National Israel, not individuals. Jesus Himself confirmed this as it is recorded in John 12:37-41. But notice John 12:42. *"Nevertheless among the chief rulers also many believed on him."* The blindness is national, not individual. Their rejection of the Messiahship of Yeshua was a national (political) act. God then set Israel, nationally, aside in order that the Gospel, which they were to receive and then share with the entire world, might go to the Gentiles. *"I say then, have they* [the Jew] *stumbled that they should fall? God forbid: but rather through their* [the Jew's] *fall salvation is come unto the Gentiles for to provoke them* [the Jews] *to jealousy."* (Rom. 11: 11). Thus God's purpose in setting aside Israel nationally was so that the Gospel could be delivered to the Gentiles in order that they in turn could take it to individual

Jews. *"For as ye* [Gentiles] *in times past have not believed God, yet have now obtained mercy through their* [the Jew's] *unbelief: even so have these* [the Jews] also *not believed, that through your* [Gentiles'] *mercy they* [the Jews] *also may obtain mercy."* (Rom. 11:30, 31). So the blindness is national (political) with a very positive Divine purpose for reaching the Jew first and also the Greek through the Gentiles who are saved by God's grace as a direct result of Israel's national blindness.

The issue, then, in Romans 11:25 is the mystery that obviously relates to National Israel and not the Church. A Biblical mystery is a truth previously unrevealed in Old Testament times that is now being revealed (Eph. 3:1-5). The conclusion of Israel's national blindness is the mystery that is here being revealed. It relates to what is to be understood as the meaning of the phrase "the fullness of the Gentiles."

God's purpose in calling Abraham and his seed was that through Israel He would be glorified among all nations. God chose Israel for several reasons: to be the repository of His revelation; to preserve that revelation; to share that revelation; and thus glorify Himself. Israel did receive and, thank God, preserve the revelation. But they did not share the revelation. The penalty for failure was a temporary expulsion from the land. This included giving the land over into Gentile hands until such time as they would return to God. And fail they did. They refused to go among the Gentiles and share the revelation. The attitude of the prophet Jonah was typical of the Jewish attitude regarding the sharing of God's revelation with those who were not Jews. Thus, by the time of Jesus, this was an attitude that went back at least seven centuries. For this, Jesus denounced the Jews in scathing terms (cf. Matt. 23:13-39). And for this, they rejected Him. Their rejection resulted in their national ejection from the land by the Romans in 70 A.D. with the land given over into Gentile hands.

The Abrahamic Covenant, dealing with the possession of the land, was then set aside "until the fullness of the Gentiles be come in," that is, until the day of the Gentiles' testing shall be finished. One of the reasons why God chose Israel was that they might be a praise unto Him. *"This people have I formed for myself; they shall show forth my praise."* (Isa. 43:21). It is interesting that the word "Jew" literally means "praise or praiser of God." That thought follows through regarding the divine purpose in salvation as stated by Paul to the Ephesians: *"That we should be to the praise of his glory, who first trusted in Christ."* (Eph. 2:12). Then speaking to Gentiles he goes on to state in the next verse; *"In whom ye also trusted, after that ye heard the word of truth, the gospel of your salvation."* If you read Romans 11:11, 30, 31 carefully, you will see that the reason why God brought salvation to the Gentiles was that through the Gentiles He might win back Abraham's seed to Himself by causing the Gentiles to provoke them, the Jews, to jealousy. In other words, God is calling out Gentiles to become members of the Church, His body, in order that these same Gentiles would share the Gospel with the Jews, bringing many back to their Messiah in order that God would be praised, as

He had originally planned, through the salvation of both Jew and Gentile!

Why has this not happened? First, it has not happened because Gentiles have become "high-minded". They began to believe that they are superior to the Jews. Thus they fell into the very trap of which Paul warned them (Rom. 11:18-21). Second, these Gentiles whom God called out to be partakers with the Jews in the spiritual blessings of the Church have essentially done the same thing that the Jews did. In turning the blessings in upon themselves they thus refused to obediently share those blessings with the Jews.

This presents a third phase of Gentile failure. Not only has the Christ-rejecting world powers abused the Jews and blasphemed God in the treading down of His Holy City, Jerusalem, but the Gentiles, who have been professed followers of Israel's Messiah, the Lord Jesus, have also failed by neglecting to keep God's command to take the Gospel message back to the Jew! Therefore, soon, the prophecy of Revelation 3:16, *"I will spue thee out of my mouth"* will be fulfilled. Why was Israel driven from her land? Was it not, among other reasons, because she refused to testify to the Gentiles? (cf. Isa. 49:6). Thus shall God also spue backslidden Christendom out of His mouth because of their refusal to testify to the Jews. Is this not Paul's message recorded in Romans 11:20-22? *"Because of unbelief they* [the Jews] *were broken off, and thou* [Gentile believers] *standest by faith. Be not high-minded, but fear: for if God spared not the natural branches, take heed lest he also spare not thee.*"

It now becomes clear that "the fullness of the Gentiles" is not an allusion to a number in God's mind of those Gentiles that must be saved before Israel's blindness is removed. It simply means that when the measure of Gentile iniquity and opportunity is full, God will again turn to the Jewish nation to carry out through them His program for this world's destiny. Consider Genesis 15:16. *"But in the fourth generation they shall come hither again: for the iniquity of the Amorites is not yet full."* In other words, God gave the Amorites a full opportunity, so that when He passed judgment upon them their iniquity was "full." Consider also Daniel 8: 23. *"And in the latter time of their kingdom, when the transgressors are come to the full, a king of fierce countenance, and understanding dark sentences, shall stand up."* Again, we have the expression "full" meaning the full measure of sins.

It has been suggested that the Greek word *pleroma* translated "fullness", is used in scripture only in connection with blessing and not with judgment. But a careful investigation will easily prove this assumption false. In addition to the references we have already quoted above consider its use in Galatians 4:4 where we read *"But when the fullness of time was come, God sent forth his Son."* There was no fullness of blessing either historically for the Jew or in the status of the Gentile world. The world was in fact in a state of corruption. As for Israel, she had reached her lowest ebb of spiritual and material decline. Obviously, *pleroma* does not mean "fullness of blessing" in this case. It simply means that Jesus came right on time according to God's sovereign schedule.

The essence of Paul's message in Romans 11:25 is that national Israel's spiritual blindness will end when the Gentile's cup of iniquity is full. Therefore, this has nothing to do with a number in God's mind of Gentiles that must be saved before Christ may return!

"And so all Israel shall be saved." (Rom. 11: 26). This speaks of the restoration of the nation of Israel both into the land and to His favor as necessitated by the New Covenant (Jer. 31:31-34). When this takes place the Church will be gone. Both the earthly and spiritual promises given to Israel will be fulfilled at once! Consider Isaiah 66: 7-9, *"Before she travailed, she brought forth; before her pain came, she was delivered of a man child. Who hath heard such a thing? Who hath seen such things? Shall the earth be made to bring forth in one day? Or shall a nation be born at once? For as soon as Zion travailed, she brought forth her children."* Verse seven is a prediction of the first coming of Israel's Messiah. The following verses predict the day when the Jewish people, as a nation, will go through a period of great travail (Daniel's 70th week), come to a place where they will recognize both their national sin of rebellion and who is their true Messiah (Zech. 12:10), repent of their sin, and receive Him as their Messiah/King. Then the nation will be re-born, that is re-established both physically and spiritually, in a moment (cf.

Zech 13:8, 9). This becomes clear in Romans 11:27. *"For this is my covenant unto them, when I shall take away their sins."* Thus it is predicted that God will go back to His covenant relation with Israel, which means a restored national relation, a re-gathering to their own land and the re-establishment of the Throne of David.

So, the phrase *"The fullness of the Gentiles"* is not predicting a number in God's mind of Gentile conversions that, when reached, will cause Him to rapture away the Church. Nor does it speak of a Gentile Church age. This phrase speaks of judgment for the Gentile nations that will occur when their cup of iniquity is full. Thus, the teaching of a Gentile Church or Gentile Church age is false and is no more than an excuse to not obediently evangelize the Jewish people.

CHAPTER FOUR

ISRAEL'S PARTIAL BLINDNESS

§§

W hat, then, is the significance of the phrase *"blindness in part is happened to Israel?"* (Rom. 11: 25b). It is strange how many Bible students skip over the words "in part." There are two ideas embodied here. First, the verse teaches that a part of the Jews are blinded, while another part, the remnant, receives the Gospel gladly (Rom. 11:17). It is interesting that the Bible teaches the very same thing about Gentiles, namely, that only a small remnant will receive the Gospel while great majorities will reject the Christ, Israel's Messiah (cf. Matt. 7:13, 14). Is it not true that the Church is composed of a remnant from all nations? The idea that the Jews are cast off because Rome, under Titus, destroyed Jerusalem is without merit. The Jewish national dispersion has no relation to the opportunity for salvation for individual Jews. The dispersion was the result of national Israel's disobedience. As we have seen, it was a national judgment. Thus it does not preclude their opportunity to be saved.

"For God so loved the world, that he gave his only begotten son, that whosoever believeth in him should not perish but have everlasting life." (John 3:16). Does not the "whosoever" include the Jew? Paul spoke of this very issue in Romans 11:7 when he wrote: *"What then? Israel hath not obtained that which he seeketh for; but the election hath obtained it, and the rest were blinded."* Even though there is presently a national blindness, so that the nation of Israel cannot repent and return to the Lord, many Jews, individually, are hearing and receiving the Word gladly This is one aspect of the fulfillment of the prophecy of "blindness in part."

Second, this concept of partial blindness embodies the idea that this national blindness is limited, that a day will come when Israel, as a nation, will recognize her sin and understand that Yeshua is, indeed, her Messiah/King. At that time Israel will repent of her national sin of rejecting the Messiah and by faith receive Him as her Messiah/Redeemer. It was Zechariah who wrote of this national redemption. *"And it shall come to pass in that day, that I will seek to destroy all the nations that come against Jerusalem. And I will pour upon the house of David, and the inhabitants of Jerusalem, the spirit of grace and supplications: and they shall look upon me whom they have pierced, and they shall mourn for him, as one mourneth for his only son, and shall be in bitterness for him, as one that is in bitterness for his first-*

born." (Zech. 2: 9, 10). Verse nine gives us the time: when God destroys the nations which come against Jerusalem. This alludes to the time when God will judge the Gentile nations. From other scriptures we know that this will take place at the end of Daniel's seventieth week. Yeshua will return in glory. Israel will recognize Him for who He is, confess her sin of rejecting Him, repent and receive Him as her Messiah/Redeemer and King (cf. Zech 13:9).

Does this mean, as some today teach, that all the Jews of every generation will be saved at this time? The answer is a resounding "No!" There are two primary passages that deal with the result of God's judgment of Israel. Zechariah 13:8, 9 makes clear that only one-third of those dwelling in the land of Israel will survive the tribulation judgment and be saved. *"And it shall come to pass, that in all the land, saith the LORD, two parts therein shall be cut off and die; but the third shall be left therein. And I will bring the third part through the fire, and refine them as silver is refined, and will try them as gold is tried: they shall call on my name, and I will hear them: I will say, it is my people: and they shall say, the LORD is my God."* In verse 7 we have the cutting off of the Messiah (cf. Jn. 10:11; Isa. 53:10; Dan. 9:26, etc.). So the judgment of verse eight takes place after Messiah is cut off. Verse nine places it just before Israel's national redemption, which will occur at the time of Messiah's return (cf. Zech. 14:1 ff). In the passage before us the Jews dwelling in the Promised Land, "eretz Israel", are the target of this judgment. Zechariah uses the term "eretz" eighteen times in his prophecy. In almost every instance it is used in the narrow sense of "a country" (cf. Zech. 9:16 as an example). Thus this judgment takes place in the land of Israel. It is interesting that most would agree with this statement but not agree that it deals <u>only</u> with those living in the Land of Israel at the time. This passage is often used to erroneously teach that all the Jews must return to the Promised Land before Messiah can return. As we shall see, this cannot be true. Consider also the means of judgment and its result according to Zechariah. In verse eight it is passing through the fire with one third surviving. This is clearly Daniel's 70th week, the period of Tribulation that immediately precedes Messiah's glorious return to establish His Millennial Kingdom. Clearly, not all Jews will be saved and brought into the Millennial Kingdom.

According to Ezekiel 20:33-38, only one tenth of those residing outside the Promised Land will survive the Great Tribulation. The key verse of this passage is verse 37: *"And I will cause you to pass under the rod, and I will bring you into the bond of the covenant."* Most Bible teachers simply state that one-third of all Jews everywhere will survive the Tribulation. But this is just not true. These two passages speak of two different judgments that take place in two different locations, yet occurring at the same time: immediately preceding the second coming of the Messiah.

Let us look closer at Ezekiel 20:33-38. Ezekiel 20: 39-42 deals with Israel's re-establishment in the land for millennial blessing. Therefore this judgment must immediately precede the second coming of the Messiah who comes to establish the Millennial Kingdom. The people who are judged here are from the Diaspora, those who have <u>not</u> returned to the Promised Land. God states: *"I will bring you out from the people, and will gather you out of the countries wherein ye are scattered."* (20: 34). We know that this does not include the Jews who dwell in Israel at this time because verse thirty-eight says of those who are judged here that: *"they shall not enter into the land of Israel."* According to Ezekiel, in verse thirty-five, this judgment takes place in a wilderness place, not in Israel. The method of judgment is stated in verse thirty-seven: *"And I will cause you to pass under the rod."* What is meant by "passing under the rod?" The scripture is its own best interpreter. Moses gives us the definition in Leviticus 27:32. *"And concerning the tithe of the herd, or of the flock, even of whatsoever passeth under the rod, the tenth shall be holy unto the LORD."* We are only interested in the term "whatsoever" because that one word takes this definition beyond its pastoral sense. This defines what is meant to "pass under the rod" as we have it in the Ezekiel passage. Ezekiel is not interested in sheep or goats. He is describing God's judgment of His people. Thus, as to pass under the rod is defined as a separation of the unholy from the holy, and as Ezekiel makes clear that only the holy will enter into the promised land to experience the Kingdom rule of the Messiah, Ezekiel teaches that the result of this particular judgment will be that only one-tenth will survive it. Matthew Henry, in his commentary on Ezekiel dealing with verses 33 to 44, writes: *There*

will come a distinguishing day, when God will sepa-
rate between the precious and the vile; he will cause
them, as the shepherd causes his sheep, to pass under
the rod when he tithes them (Lev. 27:32), that he may
mark which is for God.[1] Though not dealing with the
same time period as that of Ezekiel, the principle of
Leviticus 27:32 is illustrated by God when He stated:
"For thus saith the Lord God; the city that went out
by a thousand shall leave an hundred, and that which
went forth by an hundred shall leave ten, to the house
of Israel" (Amos 5:3). Thus, the result of this judgment must be that only one tenth will survive it, just
as in the Zechariah passage the result will be only
one third who will survive it.

So we see two different judgments of two
different groups of Jewish people taking place in
two different places, but occurring at about the same
time. Therefore, of the approximately sixteen million
Jews in the world today, if Yeshua were to come and
rapture out His Church, less than three million would
survive the tribulation long enough to recognize the
Messiah and receive Him as their Messiah/Redeemer.
What a powerful reason to share the Gospel with
the Jew now while there is yet time! But this also
gives proof that the phrase in Romans 11:25 "blindness in part" does not teach that every Jew of every
generation will be re-born and thus be included in the
Millennial Kingdom reign of their Blessed Messiah.
God help us to reach them now with the Gospel
message before it is eternally too late!

CHAPTER FIVE

IS A "GENTILE" CHURCH SCRIPTURAL?

❦❦

Let us examine one final time the teaching of Romans 11: 25 which we have already quoted. Paul has been discussing in the two preceding verses two distinct lines of truth, national rejection and individual election. The Jew is being punished nationally by a temporary suspension of the Abrahamic Covenant, a covenant that has to do with Israel's possession of the Promised Land. She was driven out and scattered over the face of the earth. This is a national punishment for a national sin.

But then a new mystery is revealed: the Church. It is established by the Lord Jesus and is a called-out body of believers composed of both Jews and Gentiles. The rule during the Church age is "Whosoever will." This we call individual election. God is not now dealing with the nation as such, whether Jewish or Gentile, but with individuals. Therefore, the fact that the Jews nationally have been set aside does not affect the opportunity of an individual Jew to become a child of God through personal faith in Messiah Jesus. Upon completion of this faith transaction the Jewish person becomes a part of the Church just as surely as does a Gentile (cf. II Cor. 3:12-16; Eph. 2:14-18).

The teaching of a Gentile Church contradicts every passage of Scripture on this point. It would mean no Jewish conversions. It would mean only an exclusive crusade among Gentiles, the general practice among most churches and general mission agencies today. That is not what the Bible teaches however. The concept of a Gentile Church is not scriptural. Neither are the resulting practices based upon it.

Second, such a concept dishonors the very character of God. Because a mob of Jews, egged on by the political henchmen of the hour, shouted, "Crucify Him!" do we think God is going to condemn uncounted and unborn millions of Jews to an irrevocable hell without even giving each individual Jew the same opportunity as each Gentile to become a child of God? No, of course not! The God of the Bible is not that kind of God! He is still the God of Grace, the God of the "whosever wills." Therefore the teaching of a "Gentile" Church is not scriptural. Neither are the practices based upon this false teaching scriptural.

Third, such a teaching invalidates all Jewish conversions, from the first disciple in Jerusalem to the very latest Jewish believer of our day. No Peter, no Paul, and no three thousand saved at Pentecost!

No early Church because most believers were Jewish. There would be no Bible because the Bible, particularly the New Testament which was humanly written by Jewish believers, would be proven false. Let us not forget that it was because there was a Jew named Paul, that Gentiles today have the hope of salvation! It is true that God is the reason we have whatever good thing we have. But Paul, a Jew, was His chosen instrument.

Neither would there be a Jewish remnant as is so clearly declared in Romans 11:5. *"Even so then at this present time also there is a remnant according to the election of grace."* "At this present time" refers to the present Church age. Obviously, Paul is pointing out that the Church is not complete without Jewish believers in it. Therefore, again, we see that the concept of a Gentile Church is not scriptural.

We are thus driven to the inescapable truth that the expressions the "Times of the Gentiles" (an era in time) and the Fullness of the Gentiles" (the climax and judgment at the end of that era) are not synonymous but related. The "Times of the Gentiles" and the "Fullness of the Gentiles" end simultaneously. The first phrase appears only once in all of Scripture, Luke 21: 24. Since this phrase has priority by about thirty years in scriptural usage, and since it is clearly defined by Jesus as having to do only with Gentile world dominion, it is consistent, when we find the almost identical expression in Romans 11:25, to realize that it means exactly the same thing as the first usage. That is especially true when we note that the settings are the same, Gentile dominion and

Jewish national restoration being directly contrasted. Scripture is always its best interpreter.

It was understood, even in the early church, that the church would be overwhelmingly Gentile in its makeup. In Acts 15:14-17 we read: *"Simeon hath declared how God at first did visit the Gentiles, to take out of them a people for his name. And to this agree the words of the prophets: as it is written, After this I will return, and will build again the tabernacle of David, which is fallen down; and I will build again the ruins thereof, and I will set it up: that the residue of men might seek after the Lord, and all the Gentiles, upon whom my name is called, saith the Lord who doeth all these things."* It is clear that, of necessity, Gentile believers would outnumber Jewish believers. It would be so even if every one of the approximately 16 million Jewish people in the world should be saved as they only make up about three percent of the total world population. However, it is clear that God's Word does not teach an exclusively Gentile Church or a Gentile Church age. God's Word teaches a church constituted of both Jewish and Gentile believers worshipping together as one (cf. Eph. 2:11-22).

CHAPTER SIX

THE CHURCH AND THE JEWISH CONNECTION

᭤᭠

One day Jesus and His disciples were traveling from Judea to Galilee. In doing so they passed through Samaria. While still in Samaria they stopped by a well. While Jesus rested, His disciples went into town to buy some food. A Samaritan woman came by to draw water and Jesus engaged her in conversation. The conversation soon turned to a religious issue: the right place to worship. It was then that Jesus made an interesting statement. He said: *"Ye worship ye no not what: we know what we worship: for salvation is of the Jews."* (Jn. 4:22). Christianity was never intended to be the "religion" of the Gentiles.

Paul makes the Jewish connection eminently clear in Romans 11: 16-18. *"For if the first fruit be holy, the lump is also holy: and if the root be holy, so are the branches. And if some of the branches be broken off, and thou, being a wild olive tree, wert graffed in among them, and with them partakest of the root and fatness of the olive tree; boast not against the branches. But if thou boast, thou bearest not the root, but the root thee,"* First, consider to whom Paul is speaking. He states: *"For I speak to you Gentiles."* (Rom. 11:13a). This letter was written to a predominantly Gentile local church. Paul was talking to Gentile believers.

Second, consider the contrast Paul draws between the true olive tree and a wild olive tree. This is a contrast between the Jewish people and Gentiles. Paul's message simply is that true religion is found in Biblical (as opposed to rabbinic) Judaism. Jews who refuse to believe are pruned out and, according to Jesus, cast into the fire (cf. Jn. 15:1-6) and burned. Gentiles, the wild olive branches, are grafted into the true olive tree the moment they put their trust in Israel's Messiah. So it is Gentiles who are grafted into the true olive tree, not Jews being grafted into a wild olive tree. In reality, what we, as Gentiles, have found is the true faith that God had shared with the Jews through Abraham, Isaac and Jacob but which they lost through rebellion against the true faith and by the addition of their traditions.

Paul goes on to point out that if Jewish people come to faith, though they were pruned out because of their unbelief, the moment they believe they are grafted back in. *"And they also, if they abide not still in unbelief, shall be graffed in: for God is able to graff them in again."* (Rom. 11:23). This indicates that Jewish people can be saved like anyone else.

Thus our message to them must be a call to return to the true faith of their fathers!

What, then, is Biblical Judaism? Biblical Judaism is the sum total of the doctrines clearly delineated in the Hebrew Bible, the Old Testament. A simple comparison of the New Testament with the Old Testament will show that every doctrine we as Christians hold dear, with the exception of the doctrine of the Church, is to be found in the Old Testament, including the doctrine of Grace. Therefore what we as Christians believe, in this sense, is very Jewish.

If God's relationship with Israel is by covenant, how do we as Gentiles fit in? The answer to this question is found in Jeremiah 31:31-35. This is the statement of the New Covenant that replaces the Mosaic Covenant (cf. Jer. 31:31-32). Moses was the first to speak to the Israelites of this new covenant that would one day replace the Mosaic Covenant (cf. Deut. 30:5-6).

It must be understood that there are two types of covenants in the Bible: conditional and unconditional. It must be further understood that all Biblical covenants are unilateral (one sided): that is from God to man, never from man to God. Each covenant has its own formula so that the reader can discern which type it is. The formula for a conditional covenant is when God states: "If you.....I will." The Mosaic Covenant is a conditional covenant. We see this in Deuteronomy 28 where God speaks of the blessings and the curses. If Israel keeps God's commandments they will be blessed. But if they fail to keep His commandments they will be cursed. History proves that God has kept his promises related to this covenant.

The formula for an unconditional covenant is when God simply states: "I will." The Abrahamic Covenant is the prime example of this type of covenant as God three times said: "I will" and never once said: "If you." (cf. Genesis 12: 1-3). An examination of the New Covenant in Jeremiah 31 brings us to the conclusion that the New Covenant is also unconditional as there is not one "if you" to be found among five "I wills".

It is to be further noted that though not all covenants of the Bible are instituted by a blood sacrifice all of the major covenants are instituted by a blood sacrifice. The Abrahamic Covenant was instituted with a blood sacrifice (cf. Gen. 15: 1-17) as was the Mosaic Covenant (cf. Ex. 24: 1-8). Thus it is safe to assume that the New Covenant which replaces another major covenant is also a major covenant and thus would be instituted by a blood sacrifice.

Scripture informs us of when this sacrifice took place. As Jesus celebrated Passover with His disciples that fateful night He broke the bread and said: *"Take eat; this is my body. And he took the cup, and gave thanks, and gave it to them, saying, Drink ye all of it; for this is my blood of the New Testament* (covenant) *which is shed for many for the remission of sins."* (Matt, 26: 27-28). When Jesus offered Himself at Calvary He offered Himself as the "Lamb of God" (Jn. 1: 29). His sacrifice put an end to the Mosaic Covenant and instituted the New Covenant. That is precisely the message of the author of Hebrews who wrote: *"Then said he, Lo, I come to do thy will, O God. He taketh away the first, that he may establish the second."* (Heb. 10: 9). This is also taught in Hebrews 8: 6-13.

Thus we, as Gentiles, are grafted into the true olive tree through the New Covenant. Christianity, then, is very Jewish. Therefore there cannot be a Gentile Church nor can there be a Gentile Church age.

CHAPTER SEVEN

THE MESSIANIC SYNAGOGUE MOVEMENT

֍֍

The false teaching of a Gentile Church has led to the rise of the Messianic Synagogue Movement. If the church is "Gentile" and yet Jews are being saved but unwelcome in the churches, what do we do with them? If God is saving Jewish people today there must be a place for them. The solution being offered by many today is the Messianic Synagogue. Is this a scripturally acceptable solution?

One emphasis of the Messianic Synagogue Movement is the continuation of many of the traditions of Rabbinic Judaism. The idea is to create and foster "the national idea" and to observe the national rites and customs of the Jews, such as keeping the Sabbath, circumcision, etc., many of which do not even have their origin in Mosaic Law. What does

Paul, who had been a staunch rabbinic teacher persecuting the early Church (Gal. 1:13-14) before being saved, say about this?

When Paul became a follower of Messiah Jesus he laid all of these traditions aside. Rather than finding his identity in his "Jewishness" he found it in the Messiah, the Lord Jesus (Phil. 3:7-11). Though he continued to recognize his Jewishness ethnically Paul went on to warn his Jewish brethren to follow his example. *"Beware lest any man spoil you through philosophy and vain deceit, after the tradition of the men, after the rudiments of the world, and not after Christ."* (Acts 13:13-41; Col. 2:8). Cf. Isa. 29:9-14.

Peter also gave a similar warning as is recorded in I Peter 1:18-19. *"Forasmuch as ye know that ye were not redeemed with corruptible things, as silver and gold, from your vain conversation received by tradition from your fathers; but with the precious blood of Christ, as of a lamb without blemish and without spot."* Even Jesus Himself attacked the tradition of the Rabbis. The Pharisees were attacking the disciples because they did not wash their hands before eating bread. Jesus answered them: *"Why do ye also transgress the commandment of God by your tradition?"* (Matt. 15:3). He pointed out that by their traditions they had made God's law of none effect (Matt. 15:1-9; Mk. 7:1-13). So we note that Paul, Peter, and even Jesus opposed the Judaizing of the Christian experience.

Another emphasis of the Messianic Synagogue Movement is the imposing of the law on believers. Of the law Paul wrote: *"Before faith came, we were kept under the law, shut up unto the faith which should afterwards be revealed. Wherefore the law was our schoolmaster to bring us unto Christ, that we might be justified by faith. But after that faith is come, we are no longer under a schoolmaster."* (Gal. 3:23-25). The scriptures teach that we are not justified by the keeping of the law but by grace through faith in Israel's Messiah, the Lord Jesus (cf. Gal. 2:16; Eph. 2:9-10). Speaking of the relationship of Jews and Gentiles Paul further states: *"But now in Christ Jesus ye who sometimes were far off* [Gentiles] *are made nigh by the blood of Christ. For he is our peace, who hath made both one, and hath broken down the middle wall of partition between us; Having abolished in his flesh the enmity, <u>even the law of commandments contained in ordinances</u>; for to make in himself of twain one new man, so making peace; And that he might reconcile both unto God in one body by the cross, having slain the enmity thereby.* (Eph. 2:13-16). Through their emphasis on the keeping of the law and the practicing of many of the traditions the Messianic Synagogue promotes divisions between Jewish and Gentile believers, not peace. Therefore as the Messianic Synagogue Movement is in clear contradiction to God's Word the movement cannot be scriptural.

What about the keeping of the Sabbath? Should not Jewish believers at least be obligated to keep the Sabbath? The answer is "No". The Sabbath was given to Israel as a unique covenant. *"Wherefore the children of Israel shall keep the Sabbath, to observe the Sabbath throughout their generations, for a perpetual covenant. It is a sign between me and the children of Israel."* (Ex. 31:16-17a). This thought is repeated in Deuteronomy 5:15 and confirmed by Ezekiel. *"Moreover also I gave them my Sabbaths, to be a sign between me and them, that they might know that I am the LORD that sanctify them...And hallow my Sabbaths; and they shall be a sign between me and you, that ye may know that I am the LORD your God."* (Ezek. 20:12, 20).

The keeping of the Sabbath is a covenant between God and National Israel. As God is not dealing with the Jews nationally in this present age, it is evident that the Sabbath is not a requirement for believing Jews in this age. As the Church is not National Israel the keeping of the Sabbath is not a requirement for Gentiles either. The Sabbath was a covenant between God and National Israel, not the Church.

As we have already noted in the previous chapter, the Mosaic Covenant (the old covenant) has already been set aside by God in favor of the New Covenant. Today God is dealing with individuals, both Jewish and Gentile, transforming their heart according to the New Covenant promises. Because this is true, Messianic Judaism, which insists on keeping much of the Mosaic system and the traditions, cannot be of God.

Further, Paul states: *"Let no man therefore judge you in meat, or in drink, or in respect of an holyday, of the new moon, or of the Sabbath days: which are shadows of things to come; but the body is of Christ"* (Col. 2:16-17). The feasts, festivals, sacrifices and holy days required under the Mosaic Covenant were but shadows of that which would become real. They were intended to point Israel to the one true Lamb of God (Messiah) who would take away all sin and bring peace with the God of Abraham, Isaac and Jacob. The Messianic Synagogue, though most local fellowships proclaim Christ as Messiah/Redeemer, emphasizes the shadows rather than the practicing of the reality thus stunting the growth of the believer. The whole emphasis of the Epistle to the Hebrews is to show that Christ is better than all of the elements of the old Mosaic system. As the Messianic Synagogue Movement emphasizes the shadows it cannot be of God.

It also must be noted that, according to Paul in Galatians 3:28, in Christ there are no ethnic, social or sexual distinctions. He writes: *"There is neither Jew nor Greek, there is neither bond nor free, there is neither male nor female: for we are all one in Christ Jesus."* So in the Church, there is no distinction between Jew and Gentile. Therefore, just as there cannot be a "Gentile" Church because there is neither Jew nor Gentile, so there cannot be a "Jewish" Church because in Christ we are all one without distinction of our ethnic, social or sexual characteristics. This does not mean that either Jews or Gentiles lose their national or ethnic heritage. It simply means that their heritage is of no consequence in the Church. Therefore the Messianic Synagogue Movement, which seeks to maintain a national/ethnic identity, is not scriptural.

Finally, what Divine covenant with Israel is replaced by the New Covenant as recorded in

51

Jeremiah 31:31, 32? Is it not the Mosaic Covenant? In verse 32 God states: *"Not according to the covenant that I made with their fathers, in the day that I took them by the hand to bring them out of the land of Egypt."* When was the New Covenant instituted? According to Jesus, as recorded in Matthew 26:26-28, it was instituted with His death at Calvary. The author of Hebrews confirms it. *"For there is verily a disannulling of the commandment going before the weakness and unprofitableness thereof. For the law made nothing perfect, but the bringing in of a better hope did; by the which we draw nigh unto God...Then said he, Lo, I come to do thy will, O God. He taketh away the first, that he may establish the second. By the which will we are sanctified through the offering of the body of Jesus Christ once for all."* Heb. 7:18, 19; 10:9. Read also Hebrews 8:7-13. If God has removed the Mosaic Covenant and replaced it with the New Covenant, to follow the things of the Old Covenant is to defy God's clear instructions. As this is what the Messianic Synagogue Movement is doing, it cannot be of God.

How tragic that the fundamental reason for the inception of the Messianic Synagogue Movement was the false idea of a Gentile Church. Yet, apart from that, Jesus, Peter and Paul all teach that the Messianic Synagogue Movement has no scriptural foundation. As we have already noted, Jewish believers are to be discipled into the Local Church just as are Gentile believers. In so doing the Local Church is blessed (cf. Gen. 12: 3; Psalm 122: 6).

CHAPTER EIGHT

ALL ISRAEL SHALL BE SAVED

ॐॐ

Some people have taken the statement *"and so all Israel shall be saved"* (Rom. 11:26) to mean that Jews from Abraham to the time of this fulfillment will all be saved. There is not one shred of evidence to support such an optimistic belief. There is no magic for those who are Jewish any more than there is for Gentiles raised in a Christian home. God's Word still states: *"There is none other name under heaven given among men, whereby we must be saved."* (Acts 4: 12). This includes the Jew. Jesus told Nicodemus *"Except a man be born again, he cannot see the kingdom of God."* (Jn. 3:3). He then went on to explain to Nicodemus what he had to do to be saved. Nicodemus was a Jew. Thus a Jewish person who dies in this present age without Christ is just as lost as a Gentile who has not received Christ as his Saviour. Nowhere does scripture teach a second chance after death. As a matter of fact the Word teaches that as a tree falls there shall it lie.

The reference under consideration is to that hour in history yet to come known as the time of Great Tribulation, the Time of Jacob's Trouble or Daniel's 70th week. When that time comes, the Church will no longer be here, having been caught up to be with the Lord. Satan, for a brief time, will reign supreme on the earth. Israel will undergo the greatest agony of all her tragic history of suffering. But God promises: *"He* (Israel/Jacob) *shall be saved* (delivered) *out of it."* (Jer. 30:7). This is what Paul had in mind as he wrote Romans 11:26.

God does not say that every Jewish person living either now, or then, will be delivered. To the contrary, Zechariah reminds us that only one third of the Jews living in the Promised Land will be delivered (cf. Zech 13:8-9). Only one tenth of the Jewish people living outside the land of Israel will be delivered according to Ezekiel 20:33 ff. as we learned earlier. Thus the burden of Jewish evangelism must lie all the heavier on the heart of the earnest child of God! Is it any wonder that Jesus wept over Jerusalem? And should not we, who claim to be the Church of Christ on earth, likewise weep and labor for their salvation as we pray on Israel's behalf?

There is another consideration that is often overlooked in this connection. The basic truth of scripture regarding God's relationship with Israel and the Jewish people may be summed up in the words of the psalmist in Psalm 67: 7. *"God shall bless us* (the Jew)*; and all the ends of the earth shall fear him."* It is only as Israel is blessed and is reconciled to God that the Gentile world will receive universal blessing. Only through a restored Israel can there be a restored world.

This principle applies to the Church itself, but to a different degree. God is not now pouring out blessings on Gentile nations as such. On the contrary, He is testing them. Neither is God pouring out blessings on the Jewish nation. He is testing Israel, as a nation, preparing it for the final events that will lead up to the return of the Messiah and His millennial reign.

What, then, is God positively doing? He is gathering out a people, made up of individuals, for His Name! These people are being gathered from Jew and Gentile alike, not just from Gentiles alone. And when they are thus gathered in, they become neither Jew nor Gentile, but a new creation in Christ. For Paul wrote: *"There is neither Jew nor Greek, there is neither bond nor free, there is neither male nor female: for ye are one in Christ Jesus...for in Christ Jesus neither circumcision availeth anything, nor uncircumcision, but a new creature."* (Gal, 3:28; 6:15).

It is only reasonable to expect that just as national Israel, when restored to God, will bring blessings to the entire Gentile world, so, when individual Jews are redeemed, blessings will redound to those who play a role in leading them to their Messiah/Redeemer as well as to the Local Church itself that receives them. This is exactly what has happened throughout the history of the church age and is still happening today. This is precisely what Paul was speaking about when he wrote: *"For if the casting away of them be the reconciling of the world, what shall the receiving of them be, but life from the dead?"* (Rom. 11: 15).

So, once again we note that the Scriptures oppose the concept that the Church age is an age for Gentile blessing. We have seen that the teaching of a Gentile Church or a Gentile Church age is false from at least three perspectives: history, example, and God's Word. It has been this erroneous teaching that has robbed the Church of its privileges with regard to the Jew. Perhaps it is time to set this false teaching aside and lay hold of the truth the Bible so clearly teaches.

CHAPTER NINE

IS GOD FINISHED WITH THE JEW?

❦❦

This is a question that has been asked in Christendom for almost two thousand years. Most Christians simply have embraced the view long held by the Roman Catholic Church. This has led many to the conclusion that the promises God made to Israel have been transferred to the Church. This is taught in Covenant, Reformed or Replacement theology. However, in making the Church Israel they have refused to accept the plain teaching of God's Word. For example, they take Jeremiah 31:31 ff (the New Covenant) and teach that it was given to the Church, not to Israel (the Jewish people). Yet, God clearly stated: *"Behold, the days come, saith the LORD, that I will make a new covenant with **the house of Israel, and with the house of Judah.**"* God does not say that He will make a new covenant with the Church. How could He? At this point in history, there was no Church with whom He could have made a previous covenant! No! God clearly states that He will make a new covenant with both the northern and southern kingdoms, the two parts of the original Davidic Kingdom. These constituted the homeland of the Jews of Jeremiah's day. Thus it is clear that the New Covenant stated in Jeremiah 31:31 ff was made with the Jews. As this has not yet been fulfilled, God cannot be finished with the Jew.

If one really thinks this through they would also have to come to the conclusion that God cannot be trusted. If God made unconditional promises to national Israel and He does not keep those promises to her, does that not make God a liar? Because the advocates of this position state that the promises were made to spiritual Israel, not national Israel, they go on to argue that the Church today is spiritual Israel. Thus God has not broken His promises to Israel at all.

So the real issue is: Did God make any unconditional promises to National Israel and the Jewish people? If He did, when and to whom did He make them? A study of the Biblical covenants reveals that God made two kinds of covenants with the Jewish people and national Israel as recorded in the Old Testament: conditional and unconditional. A covenant is a legal document. Legal documents have a formula. One can tell whether a biblical covenant is conditional or unconditional by considering the covenant formula used. The formula for a conditional covenant is when God states: "If you......I will." The Mosaic Covenant is a primary example of this kind of covenant as is clearly seen in Deuteronomy 28 where God speaks of the blessings that accrue with obedience and the curses that result from disobedience.

The formula for an unconditional covenant is when God simply states: "I will". The Abrahamic Covenant, recorded in Genesis 12:1-3, which is the basis for all of the covenants God made with Israel, is a great example. Three times God states: "I will" and not once does He say: "If you". Some would suggest that the Abrahamic Covenant is not unconditional even though the formula would so indicate. To show that God intended it to be understood as unconditional one needs only to turn to Genesis 15. Abraham questions the promise God made to him as recorded in Genesis 12: 1-3. God instructs him to prepare an animal sacrifice. After the custom of that day for the establishment of a covenant Abraham was to place the sacrifices in two opposing piles. The object was that those who were party to the covenant promises would pass between the two piles thus indicating that "If I do not keep my part of the bargain so do to me as has been done to these animals." It is interesting to note that when everything was set up to commit to the covenant God caused a sleep to fall upon Abraham (cf verse 12) and only God walked between the animal parts (verse 17) indicating that the responsibility for the fulfillment of this covenant was only upon God and not Abraham. The New Covenant recorded in Jeremiah 31:31-34 is another example of an unconditional covenant. Note again the formula. Five times God states: "I will" but never "if you". Others have suggested that this covenant was not made with national Israel. But, as we have already noted, God clearly states: *"I will make a new covenant with the house of Israel, and the house of Judah."* (Jer. 31: 31). This covenant was made with both the northern and southern Kingdoms that existed in Jeremiah's day. There is no mention of the Church here!

Some would say that the Abrahamic Covenant was not made with national Israel. That is not true as God states in the covenant: *"I will make of thee a great nation..."*. This Covenant is restated to the nation of Israel in Deuteronomy 30:1-6 and is the basis for the New Covenant recorded in Jeremiah 31. It is eminently clear in Jeremiah 31:31 that this covenant is with national Israel as God states: *"I will make a new covenant with the house of Israel, and the house of Judah."*

God made unconditional covenants with Abraham, his seed, and with national Israel. God has not yet fulfilled all of the promises embodied in these unconditional covenants made with the physical seed of Abraham. For Him to transfer those promises to another group of people other than the physical seed of Abraham makes God a liar. But God is not a liar. Those unconditional promises made in the Abrahamic, Davidic and New Covenants will one day be fulfilled with national Israel and the Jews! Thus, as God is not a liar, these promises cannot be appropriated by the Church because to do so would make Him a liar!

Paul understood this when he squarely confronted the issue in Romans Chapter eleven. *"I say then,*

Hath God cast away his people? God forbid." The Greek idiom translated "God forbid" literally means "unthinkable thought" or "impossible!" Here and in verse eleven Paul uses this idiom to point out the utter absurdity of such a thought! Why? Could it be because God made some unconditional promises to Abraham, Isaac, Jacob, David and thus to the Jewish people of every generation? The promises of the Abrahamic Covenant were unconditional as were the promises made to David in the Davidic Covenant and to the Jews in the New Covenant. All of these promises were made through Abraham, David, and Jeremiah to the physical seed of Israel, not to the Church. If God does not keep His word unconditionally to Israel and the Jewish people what hope do we as Christians have that He will keep His unconditional promise of redemption to us? So, God's unconditional promises are a clear proof that He is not finished with Israel and the Jewish people.

He then goes on in Romans chapter eleven to give three further reasons why God has not cast away his people. First, he points to his own salvation. *"For I also am an Israelite, of the seed of Abraham, of the tribe of Benjamin."* He not only points to his heritage in Abraham, but that he is also of the tribe of Benjamin. This was important because the tribe of Benjamin was the only tribe that remained faithful to Judah after the death of Solomon. Descendents of this tribe were held in very high esteem in Jesus' day. This strengthened Paul's argument that God could not be finished with the Jewish people because He saved Paul.

Further, on the Jewish holy day of Pentecost the multitude that was there were all Jews (Acts 2:5). Paul argues in Romans 11:5 that *"Even so then at this present time also there is a remnant according to the election of Grace."* Those saved on the Day of Pentecost and afterward are further proof that God is not finished with the Jew. God's promise is that there will always be a believing remnant.

Paul went on to argue the historical point that the majority of the Israelites did not believe though there was always a believing remnant. He points out that the condition of Israel has always been that only a small minority (the remnant) has believed while the vast majority has not believed. History shows that God was never moved to break His unconditional promises simply because the majority refused to believe. Again and again God reaffirmed His unconditional covenant promises with Israel. Zechariah 14 is just one of many examples of God, after pronouncing judgment upon rebellious Israel, re-affirming His unconditional covenant promises. There always has been a faithful remnant. If for no other reason God remains faithful to His covenant promises to Israel and the Jewish people because of the faithful remnant. Paul's argument is simply that, as the unbelief of the majority in the past has not canceled God's unconditional promises, the majority's rejection of Yeshua as their Messiah/Redeemer now does not and cannot cancel those promises.

Paul continues to support his statement that God is not finished with the Jew by pointing out that, although through history the majority of Abraham's seed have not believed, this unbelief never negated God's unconditional Covenant promises. Notice, in spite of their unbelief and grievous idolatry in the day of Ezekiel God renewed His unconditional promise with them when He stated: *"But I had pity for mine holy name, which the house of Israel profaned among the heathen, whither they went. Therefore say unto the house of Israel, Thus saith the Lord GOD; I do not this for your sakes, O house of Israel, but for mine holy name's sake, which ye have profaned among the heathen, whither ye went. And I will sanctify my great name, which was profaned among the heathen, which ye have profaned in the midst of them; and the heathen shall know that I am the Lord, saith the Lord GOD, when I shall be sanctified before their eyes. For I will take you from among the heathen, and gather you out of all countries, and will bring you into your own land. Then will I sprinkle clean water upon you, and ye shall be clean: from all your filthiness, and from all your idols, will I cleanse you. A new heart also will I give you, and a new spirit will I put within you: and I will take away the stony heart out of your flesh, and I will give you a heart of flesh. And I will put my spirit within you, and cause you to walk in my statutes, and ye shall keep my judgments, and do them.* (Ezek. 36:21-27).

In Romans 11:14 Paul expresses his confidence that other Jews can be saved. In verses 26-27 he teaches the restoration of the nation as per God's New Covenant promises to them (Jer. 31:31-37). All of this is clear proof that the Church is not Israel, nor Israel today the Church. If one will study the

scriptures carefully, he will find that God's promises to Israel are earthly, whereas His promises to the
Church are heavenly. Thus we have overwhelming
evidence that God is not finished with the Jew.

But you may say: "But Paul states that God
blinded them." Yes, that is true; but not all of them.
Notice what he says in verse seven: *"What then?
Israel hath not obtained that which he seeketh for:
but the election hath obtained it, and the rest were
blinded."* Not every heart was blinded. Why not?
Because some had a heart to believe!

What led to the judicial blinding of the majority?
*David saith, Let their table be made a snare, and a
trap, and a stumblingblock, and a recompense unto
them: Let their eyes be darkened, that they may not
see, and bow down their back always."* (Rom. 11:9).
Let us note several things here. First, in verse seven
Paul points out that the Jewish people have always
sought after righteousness. So their motives were
good. The problem has been that they sought for
God's righteousness in the keeping of the law. Paul
stated: *"For they being ignorant of God's righteousness, and going about to establish their own righteousness, have not submitted themselves unto the
righteousness of God."* (Rom. 10:3). Thus they were
blinded.

Second, they were so sure they were right that
they closed their minds. It is true that pride goes
before a fall. Their confidence was in the keeping
of the law and making the proper sacrifices. The
majority never grasped the principle that the feasts
and sacrifices were meant to point them to a greater

truth: that seeking to establish their own righteous-ness would never be enough. The law should have taught them that they could not keep it perfectly. The feasts and sacrifices should have taught them that only God's righteousness, offered by God as a free gift and received by faith, could make them acceptable to a holy God. Leviticus 11:44-45 made it clear that they were to be holy as God is holy. God is without sin. He is absolute holiness. Man can not attain to that holiness by his own works, but only as he by faith allows God to clothe him in His righteousness. Unfortunately, the majority did not get it.

Paul goes on to quote Psalm 69:22. This indi-cated a special privilege. The priests, according to Lev. 6:16, ate their portion of the sacrifices before God. The people also, at times, were to feast in God's presence (cf. Lev. 23:6; Deut. 12:7, 18; 14:23; 27:7). But, when the table became an end in itself rather than a joyous experience of God's presence, it became to them a snare. Is there not here a warning to Christians who come to the Lord's Table with a wrong attitude? So God's judicial blinding of the people was the result of a wrong attitude. This judi-cial blinding came as a result of their own personal sin which was the result of viewing spiritual things with the wrong attitude.

Many teach that because of this judicial blinding of the Jewish people they cannot be saved. Consider Paul's statement to the Corinthians in II Cor. 3:12-16. *"Seeing then that we have such hope, we use great plainness of speech: And not as Moses, which put a vail over his face, that the children of Israel could not steadfastly look to the end of that which is abolished: But their minds were blinded: for until this day remaineth the same vail untaken away in the reading of the old testament; which vail is done away in Christ. But even unto this day, when Moses is read, the vail is upon their heart. Nevertheless when it shall turn to the Lord, the vail shall be taken away."* The antecedent of the word "it" in verse 16 is the word "heart" at the close of verse 15. I do not know about you, but that is precisely how I was saved! Jewish people can be redeemed through the proclamation of the Gospel of Jesus Christ!

So, it becomes clear that God is neither finished with (national) Israel nor with a Jewish person individually. Though national Israel has been temporarily set aside because of their sin, Paul makes it clear that it is still God's plan that individual Jewish people be saved.

CHAPTER TEN

THE OLIVE TREE CONNECTION

⸙⸙

There is one other factor that should be considered before we complete this discussion. It is the "Olive Tree Connection" found in Romans 11:16-18. *"For if the firstfruit be holy, the lump is also holy: and if the root be holy, so are the branches. And if some of the branches be broken off, and thou, being a wild olive tree, wert graffed in among them, and with them partakest of the root and fatness of the olive tree; Boast not against the branches. But if thou boast, thou bearest not the root, but the root thee."*

First, we must determine what is meant by the first fruit and the root. There are two possible answers. The first fruits may be understood to be the first Jewish people to come to faith in Jesus as their Messiah/Redeemer who thus became the foundation (root) of the early Church. With this position the conclusion would be that as a segment of Israel is holy so shall all Israel be holy. In the second view the first fruits and the root represent the patriarchs, Abraham, Isaac and Jacob, and the believing Israel of the ancient days. Jeremiah 2:2, 3 supports this understanding: *"Thou wentest after me in the wilderness, in a land that was not sown. Israel was holiness unto the LORD and the first fruits of his increase."* Thus the lump and the Branches represent the residue of the nation, or the Jewish people as a group. I believe that the second is the true meaning here. Nothing is more natural than to call one's ancestors the root and their descendents the branches. Paul certainly indicates this in verse 28.

What, then, are the cultivated olive tree and the wild olive tree? The cultivated olive tree is Israel. The branches are thus the Jewish people. Those who refused to believe were and continue to be pruned out (broken off). This is what Jesus was talking about in John 15:1-7. Many commentators suggest that this passage speaks of the Church, but that is not correct. Jesus was speaking to Jewish people. They clearly understood "the vine" to be Israel. The psalmist wrote concerning Israel: *"Thou hast brought a vine out of Egypt."* This is precisely the message of Jeremiah also. Speaking to Israel through Jeremiah God stated: *"Yet I had planted thee a noble vine, wholly a right seed: how then art thou turned into the degenerate plant of a strange vine unto me?"* (Jer. 2:21). Again, *"Thus saith the LORD of hosts, they shall thoroughly glean the remnant of Israel as a vine..."* (Jer. 6:9a). Yet again: *"The LORD called thy name, a green olive tree, fair, and of goodly fruit: with the noise of a great tumult he hath kindled fire upon it, and the branches of it are broken."* (Jer. 11:16). A vine has no value apart from the fruit it produces. It was God's intent that Israel bear fruit to glorify His Name before the world. But Israel did not bear good fruit to God's glory. So God rejected her. *"What could have been done more to my vineyard, that I have not done in it? Wherefore, when I looked that it should bring forth grapes, brought forth wild grapes? And now go to; I will tell you what I will do to my vineyard: I will take away the hedge thereof, and it shall be eaten up; and break down the wall thereof, and it shall be trodden down, and I will lay it waste."* (Isa. 5: 4-6a). Thus the cultivated Olive tree is Israel (the Jewish people). The "true vine", according to Jesus, is the true faith embodied in Abraham, Isaac and Jacob as resident in Jesus. The essence of biblical Judaism is the coming of Messiah, first to be the sacrifice for sin (Isa. 53) and secondly to be King of Kings. Those who believe in Him are further cultivated in order to bear good fruit. Those of physical Israel who refuse to believe are pruned out and *"cast into the fire."* They are thus reserved for judgment. As the branches that are burned are removed from the vine, to suggest that this is a reference to the Church would necessitate believing that one could lose his salvation. The cultivated olive tree of which Paul speaks is Israel in whom was embodied the true faith of their Fathers.

As it is clear in verse 13 that Paul is speaking to Gentiles, the wild olive tree represents the Gentile world. Individual Gentiles are represented by the branches. Those who become believers are thus grafted in to the cultivated olive tree that they may be nourished by the true faith. As Paul understood it, that true faith was clearly recorded for our nourishment by the prophets of old in what we, today, know as the Old Testament!

From this we may draw several conclusions. There can be no Gentile Church because believing Gentiles are grafted into the faith embodied in Abraham, Isaac and Jacob. We may call this "Biblical Judaism." Let us also note that Paul clearly states that the true faith is Jewish in nature, not Gentile as is so broadly taught today even in fundamental circles. Gentile believers are warned not to think themselves better than a Jewish person, believer or not. We are reminded that the true faith is rooted in the Jewish Patriarchs, Abraham, Isaac and Jacob. God chose Israel to be the repository of His revelation to the world (Gen. 12:3). Jesus, in his confrontation with the Samaritan women as recorded in John chapter 4, stated that *"Salvation is of the Jews."* If we would develop an understanding of the Jewish roots of the Christian faith the anti-Semitism that is rampant throughout the institutional church today would disappear. And, if we would begin to emphasize the Jewishness of the Christian faith, perhaps we would find more Jewish people open to the message of Yeshua as their Messiah/Redeemer.

CHAPTER ELEVEN

WHY SHOULD WE CARE?

❦❦

We should care because the Jewish people are uniquely God's specially chosen people. It was Moses who wrote: *"For thou art a holy people unto the LORD thy God: the LORD thy God hath chosen thee to be a special people unto himself, above all people that are upon the face of the earth."* (Deut. 7:6). This is repeated in Deut. 10:14, 15. In both instances God states: *"Above all people."* But have we, the Church also been chosen? The answer is "yes." This is clearly stated by Paul in Ephesians 1:4. *"According as he hath chosen us in him before the foundation of the world, that we should be holy and without blame before him in love."* However, there is no record that the statement to Israel and the Jewish people has ever been rescinded by God. Does this constitute a contradiction? Absolutely not! In Deuteronomy God states that the Jewish people are chosen *"above all people."* That simply implies order. Israel and the Jewish people have a unique place with God as an earthly people, distinct from the Church.

However, we must understand that they were not chosen for honor but for service. *"The LORD did not set his love upon you, nor choose you, because ye were more in number than any people; But because the LORD loved you, and because he would keep his oath which he had sworn unto your fathers, hath the LORD brought you out with a mighty hand, and redeemed you out of the house of bondmen, from the hand of Pharaoh king of Egypt."* (Deut. 7:7-8). First, note the re-affirmation of God's commitment to keep His unconditional covenants with the seed of Abraham, Isaac and Jacob. Second, note that God's choice gave them no cause for pride. He chose them for a very clear purpose which He covenanted to fulfill in and through them. We should care because they are God's specially chosen people.

We should also care because God uniquely loves the Jewish people. In Isaiah 49:12 God reassures Israel, at a time when he was severely judging them, of future blessing as He had promised. They responded in the following verse by asking how that could be. Note God's answer: *"Can a woman forget her sucking child, that she should not have compassion on the son of her womb? Yes, they may forget, yet will I not forget thee. Behold, I have graven thee upon the palms of my hands; thy walls are continually before me."* (Isa. 49: 15-16). God loves the Jewish people so very much that He has even written their individual names on the palms of His hands! If we are God's children and thus possess His heart, should we not also care because He loves them so much?

We should care because Jewish people can be saved (Rom. 11:14,15; II Cor. 3:13-16, etc.); because there is only one way to be saved; and because God has given to us the message of redemption with the command to share it with everyone. Note the words of Peter to the religious leaders in Jerusalem as recorded in Acts: 10:8-12. *"Then Peter, filled with the Holy Ghost, said unto them, Ye rulers of the people, and elders of Israel, If we this day be examined of the good deed done to the impotent man, by what means he is made whole; Be it known unto you all, and to all the people of Israel, that by the name of Jesus Christ of Nazareth, whom ye crucified, whom God raised from the dead, even by him doth this man stand here before you whole. This was the stone which was set at nought of you builders, which is become the head of the corner. Neither is there salvation in any other: for there is none other name under heaven given among men, whereby we must be saved."* The account of Pentecost in Acts chapter two records the salvation of about three thousand Jewish souls. In His final words our Lord stated: *"But ye shall receive power, after that the Holy Ghost is come upon you: and **ye shall** be witnesses unto me both in Jerusalem, and in all Judea, and in Samaria, and unto the uttermost parts of the earth."* (Acts 1:8). The majority of the residents of Jerusalem and Judea were Jews. The people in Samaria were the despised people. We are commanded ("Ye shall") to take the Gospel to the Jews, to those whom we may despise and to the whole world! We should care because we are so commanded by our precious Lord to do so.

We should care because God promised to bless those who care and curse those who don't. In the first unconditional covenant with Abraham and his seed God stated: *"And I will bless them that bless thee, and curse him that curseth thee: and in thee shall all families of the earth be blessed."* (Gen. 12:3). But you protest: "How have I cursed the seed of Abraham?" Do you not condemn them to hell by your refusal to share the Gospel with them? What greater curse could there be?

God has commanded: *"Pray for the peace of Jerusalem; They shall prosper that love thee."* (Psa. 122:6). There are special blessings that accrue to those who love what God loves. Already the world has been blessed through Abraham's seed, the Lord Jesus Christ. Now He has instructed us to carry the Gospel back to them. Speaking to Gentiles Paul wrote: *"For as ye in times past have not believed God, yet have now obtained mercy through their* (the Jews') *unbelief: Even so have these also now not believed, that through your mercy they (the Jews) also may obtain mercy."* (Rom. 11:30, 31). We should care because God has promised special blessing to those who do.

We should care for at least four reasons: because: They are God's uniquely chosen people above all people on the face of the earth; They are uniquely loved by God above all others; They can be saved and we have the message; and God has promised special blessings to those who do and curse to those who do not.

CHAPTER TWELVE

WHO IS RESPONSIBLE?

৪৬

What we have seen thus far is that God is not finished with the Jew. The Gospel is to both Jew and Gentile. Both are redeemed by the same Gospel (II Cor. 3:12-16). Both are to be brought into a Local Church (the believing body) (Eph. 2:14-16), not a Messianic Synagogue.

We have also noted that God's Word clearly gives no room for a "Gentile Church" or "Gentile Church Age". Neither does God's Word teach a Jewish Church or a Jewish Church Age. The Messianic Synagogue Movement has no Biblical support as is clearly seen in the books of Galatians, Ephesians and Hebrews. Both Jew and Gentile are to be discipled into a sound Bible believing Local Church (Eph. 2:16).

We have further noted that God is not finished with the Jew. Even though there is presently a "national" blindness, so that the nation of Israel cannot repent and return to the Lord, many Jews, individually, are hearing and receiving the Word gladly.

But, perhaps, the greatest lesson to be learned from God's Word on this subject is that we, as Gentiles, are grafted into the true faith (Rom. 11:13-17), not Jewish people grafted into a Gentile faith. If the Gospel is a very Jewish Gospel then it makes sense that we are to take it to the Jewish people first as the early church did and as Paul so clearly instructed.

Who, then, is responsible for getting the Gospel out to Jewish people? Our Lord's final words were these: *"But ye shall receive power after that the Holy Ghost is come upon you: and ye shall be witness unto me both in Jerusalem, and in all Judea, and in Samaria, and unto the uttermost parts of the earth."* (Acts 1:8). The early believers understood that commission to reach **all** people with the responsibility to establish local Churches who in turn would reach out to **all** people. That **"all"** includes the Jew. Thus it is the responsibility of the Local Church to evangelize the Jew just as it is the responsibility of the local church to evangelize the Gentile. In this process of reaching both Jew and Gentile, missionary agencies exist only to assist Local Churches in fulfilling this Great Commission.

The problem that confronts us today is a theology that teaches two untruths. First, it teaches a Gentile Church and/or Church age. This has affected how pastors and Local Churches look at any responsibility to share the Gospel with Jewish people as well as their view of present day Israel. Today, few fundamental church-planting missionary agencies even take the time to encourage their missionaries to include reaching out to the Jewish people, let alone training them in the verities of effectively witnessing to them. The Jewish roots of the Faith and our obligation to share the Gospel with the Jewish people are almost totally overlooked in our fundamental Bible Colleges and Seminaries today.

Second, this theology teaches that God is finished with the Jew, or at best, that they are very difficult to reach. The latter idea has not stopped Local Churches from sending missionaries to the Muslims, the Mormons, and other groups teaching false religions, which are considered difficult to reach. Some years ago, in a meeting of fundamental mission agency leaders, I asked the question of a man who was responsible for his agency's church planting ministries what they were doing to reach the Jews in the areas of their church plants. His answer to me was that "you cannot build churches witnessing to Jews!" That, of course, is not the issue. The issue is being faithful to God's command to share the Gospel. But it does express a general attitude.

If God has promised there would always be a believing remnant (and He has) and He has committed to the Local Church the responsibility to reach with the Gospel all that are lost (and He has), the Local Church must, of necessity, be responsible for sharing the Gospel with Jewish people even in our day. The Scriptures are clear. The Gospel *"Is to the Jew first, and also to the Greek."* (Rom. 1:16). This verse teaches three very import things:

1. Everyone, Jew or Gentile, who believes the gospel will be saved. (This agrees with Jesus' statement recorded in John 3:16, 18).
2. Historically, the Gospel was given to the Jew first. (Peter confirmed this as recorded in Acts 3:25-26).
3. The word *"first"* also indicates rank or order. (Paul indicates this in Romans 2:9-10). This is also in accord with God's statement recorded in Deuteronomy 7:6 and 10:15.

These three thoughts were put together by Paul in Antioch: *"It was necessary that the word of God should first have been spoken to you; but seeing you put it from you, and judge yourselves unworthy of everlasting life, lo, we turn to the Gentiles."* (Acts 13:46). The word *"necessary"* literally means "indispensable" or "required", indicating with the word *"first"* not only historical order but continuing rank. The final phrase confirms this. When the Gospel is rejected by the Jew, then it is to be taken to the Gentile. Paul thus affirms that it was right and proper that the Jews should have the first opportunity of hearing and believing the Good News. His practice of announcing the Gospel message first in the Synagogue of each city he visited was a practical expression of the principle he laid down in Romans 1:16, again confirming that the rank or order was intended. As to preference, there is none. As to method of approach, it is still to the Jew first. God has never canceled this program for missions. Is it not time for the Church to become obedient to God's method for world evangelization?

Second, because Jewish people are reachable, we must reach them. Paul said: *"Hath God cast away His people? God forbid. For I am an Israelite, of the seed of Abraham, of the tribe of Benjamin."* (Rom. 11:1). The early Church was almost totally Jewish. Paul, speaking about the Jews, wrote: *"But their minds were blinded: for until this day remaineth the same vail untaken away in the reading of the Old Testament; which vail is done away in Christ."* (II Cor. 3:14). In verse 16 Paul explains the process: *"Nevertheless when it* (the heart) *shall turn to the Lord, the vail shall be taken away."* Jewish people today may be effectively reached with the Gospel when that Gospel is properly presented to them. Therefore, the Local Church is responsible for sharing the Gospel with them. Remember, to withhold the Gospel from them is to condemn them to hell, leaving us accountable (cf. Ezek. 3:18). The ONLY way we can stand one day in His presence with clean hands is to share the Gospel with the Jewish people.

Jewish people may have many characteristics that are unlovable. But don't we all? Of the Jewish people God has said: *"I have loved thee with an everlasting love."* (Jer. 31:3). Should we who claim to have God's heart love them any less? What a special privilege it is to lovingly share the Gospel message with those who are kin to our Saviour! When we arrive home and stand in His presence what a blessing it will be to hear Him say: *"Well done, thou good and faithful servant. Inasmuch as ye have done it unto the least of these my brethren, ye have done it unto me!"* (Matt. 25:21a, 40b).

Endnotes:

§§

[1] William R. Newell. *Romans, Verse By Verse* (Chicago: Moody Press, 1938) p 22

[2] Matthew Henry, *Commentary on the Whole Bible* (Grand Rapids: Zondervan Publishing House, 1961) p 1057

BIBLIOGRAPHY

§§

Bruce, F. F.*Commentary On The Book Of Acts*. Grand Rapids: Wm. B. Eerdmans Publishing Co., 1954

Enns, Paul P.,*Ezekiel*; Grand Rapids: Zondervan Publishing House, 1986

Feinberg, Charles L, *The Prophecy Of Ezekiel;* Chicago: Moody Press, 1969

Hendriksen, William, *New Testament Commentary; Exposition of the Gospel According To Luke.* Grand Rapids: Baker Book House, 1978

Henry, Matthew, *Matthew Henry' Commentary;* Grand Rapids: Zondervan Publishing House, 1961

Hodge, Charles, *Commentary of the Epistle to the Romans.* Grand Rapids: Wm. B. Eerdmans Publishing Co., 1964

Ironside, H. A., *Addresses On The Gospel Of John* New York: Loizeaux, 1942

Kreloff, Steven A., *God's Plan For Israel, A Study Of Romans 9 – 11,* Neptune: Loizeaux, 1995

Luther, Martin, *Commentary On Romans.* Grand Rapids: Kregel Publications, 1976

Newell, William R., *Romans Verse By Verse.* Chicago: Moody Press, 1938

Pentecost, J. Dwight, *Things To Come,* Grand Rapids: Dunham Publishing Company, 1958

Showers, Renald, E., *The Most High God,* Bellmawr: Friends Of Israel Gospel Ministry, 1982

Stevens, Charles, *What It Has Cost The Church To Withhold Christ From The Jews*, Buffalo: JAM Inc. 1996

Walvoord, John F., *Daniel, The Key To Prophetic Revelation,* Chicago: Moody Press, 1971

Walvoord, John F., *Matthew, Thy Kingdom Come,* Chicago: Moody Press, 1974

Printed in the United States
201124BV00002B/343-1524/P
9 781604 775402